Carpe Cocoa, Seize the Chocolate!

40 Recipes to Celebrate Chocolate -
Sweet and Spicy; Bark, Bites, Dips,
Sauces, Truffles Treats

BY

Daniel Humphreys

License Notes

Table of Contents

Introduction

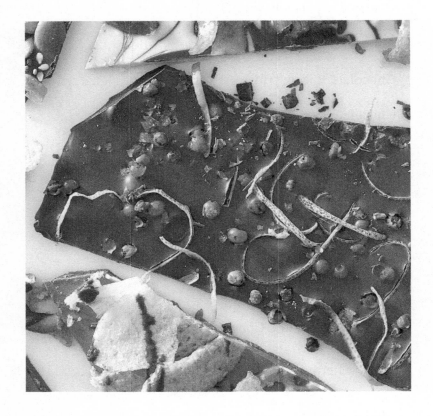

When you smell chocolate, your brain releases more theta waves which act as a relaxation trigger, so it's hardly surprising that collectively Americans consume 100 pounds of chocolate every single second.

We can reduce our risk of heart disease by 30 percent by eating dark chocolate every day.

Surprisingly, tests show that dark chocolate, in moderation, of course, can help to protect our teeth against decay.

What's more chocolate may even be more effective than codeine when it comes to combating a cough.

It isn't just dark chocolate either that is getting a good rep! Researchers at a university in Scotland reveal, that by eating 3 ½ ounces of milk chocolate once a day your chances of death from heart disease decreases by a whopping 25 percent.

Our 40 recipes will inspire you to share your chocolate creations with other like-minded chocolate lovers out there!

Happy National Chocolate Holiday; whichever ones you decide to celebrate!

Barks and Bites

Basic Chocolate Bark

Use this recipe as your basic bark and add your favorite toppings.

Servings: 3-4 cups

Total Time: 2hours 15mins

Ingredients:

- 1 (12 ounce) bag milk choc chips
- 1 tbsp. vegetable oil
- Toppings of choice

Directions:

1. Line a 10x15" cookie sheet with parchment.

2. Add the choc chips to a microwave-safe bowl.

3. Add the oil and heat the chocolate on half power, in 30-second intervals, stirring each time, until the chocolate melts and is smooth.

4. Evenly spread the chocolate on the parchment paper.

5. Top with chosen toppings.

6. Transfer to the fridge to chill.

Cardamom and Milk Chocolate Filo Bites

These little spicy bites are good enough to serve as an appetizer or after-dinner nibble. If you aren't a fan of cardamom, why not experiment with other spices?

Servings: 18 bites

Total Time: 10mins

Ingredients:

- 3½ ounces slab milk chocolate (divide into 18 equal pieces)
- 18 (4x8") filo pastry sheets
- Butter (for frying)
- ¾ tsp cardamom powder
- Fresh seasonal fruit
- Mint leaves (to garnish)

Directions:

1. Arrange one piece of chocolate on each sheet of filo. Roll, each sheet into a square-shaped egg roll.

2. Wet a clean finger and wipe it along the edges of the pastry to help adhere and bind.

3. Over moderate to low heat, melt the butter, making sure it doesn't burn.

4. In batches, if necessary, fry the 18 chocolate bites, flipping over every 20 seconds or so, until they are golden on all sides, and lightly browned. This will take no more than 60 seconds.

5. While the chocolate bites are still hot, scatter with cardamom powder, garnish with your favorite fruit and mint leaves.

Chocolate and Almond Berry Bites

Crunchy bites to satisfy your chocolate cravings.

Servings: 12 (1") bites

Total Time: 1hour 15mins

Ingredients:

- 10-12 ounces high-quality semisweet choc chips
- 1 tbsp. coconut oil
- ¼ cup almonds (chopped)
- ¼ cup dried blueberries (chopped)
- Chopped almonds (to garnish)

Directions:

1. Add the choc chips together with the coconut oil to a microwave-safe bowl and on high, in 20-second intervals, melt the chocolate.

2. Add the chopped almonds and dried blueberries and stir well to combine evenly.

3. Transfer the mixture, using a spoon, to a 12-hole silicone mold, filling each hole only halfway.

4. Transfer to the fridge for an hour until solid.

5. Remove the bites from the mold and serve.

Dark Chocolate Frozen Banana Bites

Decadent yet healthy, little frozen banana bites make perfect snacks for kids.

Servings: 12-14 bites

Total Time: 1hour 25mins

Ingredients:

- 2 ripe bananas (peeled, cut into 1" slices)
- ¾ cup dark choc chips
- Chopped peanuts (to garnish)

Directions:

1. Freeze the banana slices for an hour.

2. In a double boiler, melt the choc chips until silky.

3. Take the bananas out of the freezer and dip in the melted chocolate, immediately. Transfer to wax paper.

4. Scatter with crushed peanuts and transfer to the freezer for several minutes, or until you are ready to enjoy,

Dark Chocolate Peppermint Bark

Peppermint is usually associated with the holidays but his bark is perfect all year round.

Servings: 10-12 people

Total Time: 15mins

Ingredients:

- 12 ounces high-quality dark chocolate (roughly chopped)
- ½ tsp peppermint essence
- 5 candy canes (coarsely chopped)

Directions:

1. Set a baking sheet lined with parchment paper to one side.

2. Using a double boiler, melt the chocolate, gently stirring until melted.

3. Take off the heat and add the peppermint essence.

4. Pour the chocolate mixture onto the parchment paper and using a wooden spoon or spatula, evenly spread.

5. Sprinkle with the crushed candy canes, lightly pressing to adhere.

6. Transfer to the freezer to harden; this will take several minutes

7. Break the bark into random pieces and serve.

Date and Oat Chocolate Bites

Delicious little oatmeal balls for when you need a quick energy boost.

Servings: 16 bites

Total Time: 15mins

Ingredients:

- 12 dates (pitted)
- 1 cup oats
- 3 tbsp. coconut oil (melted)
- 3 tbsp. cocoa powder
- 2 tbsp. brewed coffee (cold)
- ½ tsp vanilla essence
- Pinch salt
- Desiccated coconut

Directions:

1. Add the dates, oats, coconut oil, cocoa powder, coffee, vanilla essence, salt and coconut to a food blender and process until combined.

2. Lightly oil clean hands and roll the dough out into small, evenly sized balls, around the size of a small cherry.

3. Roll each ball in the coconut and transfer to the refrigerator for 20 minutes to firm them up.

Decadently Dark Chocolate Bark with Pretzels

A little of this bark will go a long way.

Portions: 32 pieces

Total Time: 5hours 30mins

Ingredients:

- 1 pound high-quality dark chocolate (coarsely chopped)
- 1 cup pretzels (coarsely chopped)
- Himalayan pink salt

Directions:

1. Take a baking sheet and line it with parchment. Allow plenty of overhang.

2. Using a double boiler, melt the chocolate, stirring to combine. Take off the heat.

3. Pour the melted dark chocolate onto the parchment paper, spreading to a ¼" thickness, evenly using a spatula, while making sure you leave a border of parchment all the way around.

4. Scatter the chopped pretzels and salt over the top, lightly pressing to adhere.

5. Put to one side, to set for 4-5 hours at room temperature.

6. When set, peel the paper away from the bark and break into random pieces.

Dried Fruit Chocolate Bark

Fruity, chewy, and crunchy chocolate bark to pop in your lunchbox.

Portions: 24 pieces

Total Time: 2hours 30mins

Ingredients:

- 8 ounces bittersweet chocolate (finely chopped)
- 8 ounces semisweet chocolate (finely chopped)
- 1 cup dried apricots (chopped)
- 1 cup whole roasted, salted cashews
- ½ cup dried cranberries

Directions:

1. First, melt the chocolate s in a double boiler, stirring until totally melted.

2. Line a cookie sheet with parchment.

3. Take a ruler, and a pencil, draw a 9x10" rectangle on the parchment paper. Place the paper facing downwards on the cookie sheet.

4. Carefully pour the melted chocolate over the parchment paper, spreading it to make a rectangle, using the outline.

5. Scatter with dried apricots, salted cashews, and cranberries.

6. Put to one side to set.

7. Cut the chocolate bark into 1x3" pieces and serve.

Pink Chocolate Bark with Chipotle and Pistachios

Pretty pink, white and dark chocolate bark that looks as good as it tastes is great for a party.

Portions: 10-12

Total Time: 1hour 20mins

Ingredients:

- 12 ounces dark chocolate wafer
- 1½ tsp chipotle chili powder
- 12 ounces pink melting chocolate wafers
- 6 ounces white melting chocolate wafers
- ½ cup pistachios (chopped)
- Flaked sea salt (for sprinkling)

Directions:

1. Line an 8" square baking pan with parchment.

2. Melt the dark chocolate wafers using a double boiler. Add the chili powder and stir to combine.

3. Pour the mixture into the baking pan, making sure that the chocolate reaches the edges while tapping gently to even out the chocolate.

4. Transfer to the refrigerator to firm, around 20-30 minutes.

5. Using the double boiler method again, melt the pink chocolate wafers and white chocolate wafers separately.

6. As soon as the chocolates melt, remove the pan from the fridge and pour 75 percent of the pink chocolate over the dark. Next, drizzle the white over the pink, leaving a little of the pink chocolate exposed.

7. Scatter with pistachios and using a butter knife swirl the chocolates together.

8. Sprinkle with sea salt and additional chili powder if required.

9. Transfer to the fridge to harden, for around 20 minutes.

10. Break the bark into random pieces and enjoy.

Raspberry Rose Tea and Almond Bark

White chocolate rose tea, raspberries and almonds make a sophisticated and visually pleasing bark to share.

Portions: 16-20 pieces

Total Time: 4hours 20mins

Ingredients:

- 16 ounces white chocolate (chopped, divided)
- 1 tbsp. Raspberry Rose Hibiscus tea (divided)
- ¼ cup dried whole raspberries

- ¼ cup roasted almonds (roughly chopp
- ½ tsp pink Himalayan salt

Directions:

1. Line a cookie sheet with parchment.

2. Melt together ¾ of the chocolate, and ½ tbsp. rose tea using a double boiler.

3. Stir until the chocolate until it is melted. Take off the heat.

4. Add the remaining white chocolate until melted,

5. Pour the chocolate over the parchment and using a spatula, spread it into a rectangle.

6. Scatter the remaining tea over the wet chocolate along with the raspberries, and almonds. Scatter with sea salt.

7. Allow the mixture to sit for 2-4 hours at room temperature, or until the chocolate sets.

8. Cut into pieces and enjoy

Raspberry, Oats Dark Chocolate Bites

These bites are perfect for breakfast or a mid-morning snack.

Servings: 16 bites

Total Time: 15mins

Ingredients:

- 1 cup rolled oats
- ½ cup almonds
- ¼ cup steel cut oats

- ¼ cup raw honey
- 2-4 tbsp. unsweetened almond milk
- ¼ cup dark chocolate chips
- ⅓ cup chopped raspberries

Directions:

1. In a processor, blend the rolled oats with the almonds, and cut oats until fine.

2. Add the raw honey, and pulse until the mixture is sticking together.

3. Add the milk, a tablespoon at a time, until you achieve your preferred consistency. The mixture should be a little sticky.

4. Fold in the chocolate chips along with the raspberries.

5. Roll the mixture into 16 balls and transfer to the freezer for several minutes.

6. Enjoy.

Rocky Road Milk Chocolate Bark

A quick and easy bark recipe, ready in under an hour.

Servings: 16-18

Total Time: 45mins

Ingredients:

- 16 ounces good-quality semisweet chocolate (finely chopped)
- 1 cup mini mallows
- 1 cup walnuts (coarsely chopped)

Directions:

1. Line a cookie sheet with parchment and set to one side.

2. In a double boiler, melt the chocolate, stirring until smooth. Take off the heat and set to one side to cool for 2-3 minutes, occasionally stirring.

3. Add the mini mallows and chopped walnuts and stir to incorporate.

4. Spread the mixture onto the parchment, to cover an 8" square space.

5. Transfer to the fridge for half an hour, or until set.

6. Take a sharp knife and cut the bark into pieces, and enjoy.

Sour Cherry and Spicy Ginger Chocolate Bark

This sour and spicy bark is the perfect way to end a meal.

Servings: 16

Total Time: 45mins

Ingredients:

- 12 ounces 70% dark chocolate (chopped)
- 1 cup unsweetened dried sour cherries
- 1 cup unsalted raw almond pieces (toasted)
- ¼ cup crystallized ginger (chopped)
- Pinch kosher salt

Directions:

1. Line a rimmed sheet with aluminum foil and set to one side.

2. In a double boiler, melt the chocolate, while frequently stirring, until smooth and totally melted, around 5-6 minutes.

3. Pour the melted chocolate onto the rimmed sheet, and spread to around a ¼" thickness.

4. Scatter with sour cherries, almonds, chopped ginger and a pinch of kosher salt.

5. Chill until the chocolate is set, for around half an hour.

6. Peel off the aluminum foil and break the bark into random pieces.

White Chocolate Bark with Pomegranates and Almonds

Creamy white bark scattered with pomegranate arils and toasted almonds.

Servings: 6

Total Time: 20mins

Ingredients:

- ⅔ cup pomegranate arils
- ½ cup slivered almonds
- 1 cup milk chocolate chips
- 1 cup white chocolate chips
- 2 tsp canola oil

Directions:

1. Rinse and using kitchen towel, gently dry the pomegranate arils.

2. Next, lightly toast the almonds by placing them in the oven and baking at 325 degrees F, for 2-3 minutes, while frequently stirring.

3. Line a cookie sheet with parchment.

4. Melt milk chocolate chips together with 1 teaspoon oil, stirring often.

5. Evenly spread the melted chocolate over the middle of the paper.

6. Scatter 50 percent of the arils along with the toasted almonds over the top of the chocolate.

7. Melt the white chocolate chips and the remaining 1 tsp of canola oil, frequently stirring, until melted.

8. Using a tablespoon, drop over the milk chocolate.

9. Carefully, smooth the white chocolate over the surface.

10. Scatter with the remaining arils and almonds, gently pressing down and chill until the chocolate is set,

11. Break the bark into random chunks.

Dips and Sauces

Amaretto Cherry Dip with Milk Choc Chips

An enticing dip made with amaretto almond liqueur, which smells as wonderful as it tastes!

Servings: 4-6

Total Time: 10mins

Ingredients:

- 8 ounces full-fat cream cheese (at room temperature)
- 2 tbsp. amaretto almond liqueur
- ½ cup confectioner's sugar
- ¼ cup milk choc chips
- ⅓ cup maraschino cherry halves

Directions:

1. Beat together the cream cheese, amaretto, and confectioner's sugar until smooth.

2. Fold in the choc chips and cherry halves.

3. Serve straight away.

Aztec Hot Fudge Sundae Sauce

Give your hot fudge sundae sauce an Aztec twist with a generous pinch of cinnamon and cayenne.

Servings: 12-14

Total Time: 10mins

Ingredients:

- 4 ounces unsweetened chocolate (chopped)
- 1 cups white sugar
- ¼ cup unsalted butter
- ½ cup whole milk
- ½ tsp cinnamon
- ½ tsp vanilla essence
- Pinch kosher salt
- Generous pinch cayenne pepper

Directions:

1. In a small saucepan over moderately low heat melt together the chocolate, sugar, and butter. Stir until silky smooth.

2. Pour in the milk and stir while heating for another few minutes.

3. Take off the heat and stir in the cinnamon, vanilla, salt, and cayenne.

4. Serve hot/warm.

Boozy Dark Chocolate Mint Sauce

This boozy dark chocolate sauce gets its minty flavor form crème de menthe liqueur. Serve affogato-style, poured over a scoop of ice cream in a coupe glass.

Servings: 6

Total Time: 10mins

Ingredients:

- 1 cup heavy cream
- 1 cup whole milk
- ⅔ cup good quality dark choc chips
- 1 tbsp. cocoa powder (unsweetened)
- 1 tbsp. white sugar
- ¼ cup crème de menthe liqueur
- Chocolate ice cream (for serving)

Directions:

1. In a small saucepan heat the cream and milk together over moderately low heat.

2. Transfer the mixture to a blender along with the choc chips, cocoa powder, sugar, and liqueur. Blitz until combined.

3. Scoop chocolate ice cream into glasses and pour over the sauce.

4. Serve!

Brandy Spiked White Chocolate Dip

A real winter warmer; brandy-spiked, white chocolate sauce will have you feeling all warm and fuzzy.

Servings: 12-14

Total Time: 10mins

Ingredients:

- ½ cup half half
- ½ cup salted butter
- ½ cup white sugar
- 4 ounces white chocolate (chopped)
- 3 tbsp. brandy

Directions:

1. In a small saucepan over medium heat bring the half half, butter, and sugar to a boil, stirring until the sugar dissolves. Turn the heat down low and simmer for 5-6 minutes.

2. Take off the heat and immediately add the chopped chocolate.

3. Stir in the brandy until silky smooth.

4. Serve hot/warm.

Brown Sugar Pecan Dip with German Chocolate

This enticing dip made with brown sugar, pecans, and chocolate is guaranteed to be the star of the show at your next party or gathering.

Servings: 12-14

Total Time: 10mins

Ingredients:

- 1 cup light brown sugar
- 8 ounces full-fat cream cheese
- ½ cup German choc chips
- ½ cup pecans (chopped)
- ¾ cup coconut flakes
- Apples (cored, thinly sliced, for serving)

Directions:

1. Beat the brown sugar and cream cheese together until fluffy.

2. Fold in the German milk choc chips, chopped pecans, and coconut flakes.

3. Serve with apple slices.

Cayenne Spiced Dark Chocolate Dipping Sauce

This decadent dark chocolate dip is spiced with cayenne pepper for a sweet, fiery dip perfect for crackers, fruit, and cookies.

Servings: 3-4

Total Time: 10mins

Ingredients:

- 2 tsp cayenne pepper
- 1 cup dark choc chips
- 2 tbsp. salted butter
- 1 cup heavy cream
- Fruit, crackers, cookies (for dipping)

Directions:

1. In a medium saucepan over low heat, melt together the cayenne pepper, choc chips, butter, and cream, stirring frequently.

2. Pour into a dipping bowl and serve with fruits and crackers.

Dark Stout Beer Ice Cream Sauce

Dark stout beer gives this rich chocolate sauce a dark malty flavor. We recommend pouring over classic vanilla ice cream to let the flavor stand out.

Servings: 3-4

Total Time: 10mins

Ingredients:

- ¼ cup cocoa powder (unsweetened)
- ½ cup granulated sugar
- ½ cup dark stout beer
- 1 tsp vanilla essence
- Pinch kosher salt
- ¾ cup 60% cocoa chocolate (chopped)

Directions:

1. Bring to a boil, the cocoa powder, sugar, beer, vanilla, and salt in a small saucepan.

2. Turn the heat down low and simmer for 5-6 minutes.

3. Take off the heat and stir in the chopped chocolate, until it melts.

4. Enjoy hot/warm!

Dreamy White Chocolate Sauce

This dreamy and versatile sauce uses only three ingredients; chocolate, cream, and butter. Simply heavenly when served with fresh berries for dipping.

Servings: 3-4

Total Time: 10mins

Ingredients:

- ½ cup cream
- 2 tsp unsalted butter
- 8 ounces good-quality white chocolate. (roughly chopped)
- Fresh berries (for serving)

Directions:

1. In a small pan over moderate heat bring the cream to a boil.

2. Take off the heat and immediately add the butter and chopped chocolate.

3. Stir until silky smooth.

4. Serve hot/warm with fresh berries.

Hazelnutty Cheesecake Dip

Friends and family will go nuts for this thick cheesecake dip flavored with chocolate hazelnut spread.

Servings: 6

Total Time: 10mins

Ingredients:

- 1 cup heavy cream
- 3 tbsp. powdered sugar
- 8 ounces full-fat cream cheese (softened)
- ½ cup hazelnut chocolate spread

Directions:

1. Whip up the heavy cream until it can hold stiff peaks. Set to one side.

2. Beat together the powdered sugar, cream cheese, and hazelnut chocolate spread until whippy.

3. Fold in the whipped cream until incorporated.

4. Enjoy straight away.

Maple Greek Yogurt Dip

Grab some graham crackers and get dunkin' them in this maple chocolate dip with tangy Greek yogurt.

Servings: 8-10

Total Time: 10mins

Ingredients:

- 1 cup full-fat plain Greek yogurt
- 3 tbsp. cocoa powder (unsweetened)
- 1 tbsp. maple syrup
- ¼ tsp vanilla essence
- 3 tbsp. dark choc chips
- Graham crackers (for serving)

Directions:

1. Whisk together the yogurt, cocoa powder, maple syrup, and vanilla essence until smooth.

2. Fold in the choc chips and serve straight away with graham crackers.

Mocha Sauce

This smooth mocha delight combines the flavors of chocolate and coffee for a sauce that is guaranteed to make any dessert extra special.

Servings: 12-14

Total Time: 10mins

Ingredients:

- 1 cup semisweet chocolate (chopped)
- ¼ cup salted butter
- 1½ tbsp. espresso powder
- ¾ tsp vanilla essence
- 1 tbsp. heavy cream

Directions:

1. Melt together the chocolate, butter, espresso powder, and vanilla using a double boiler.

2. Stir in the cream and heat until warmed through.

3. Serve straight away.

Peanut Butter Cookies n Crème Dip

A sinfully good combination of all our favorite things; peanut butter, cookies n crème and, of course, chocolate.

Servings: 4-6

Total Time: 20mins

Ingredients:

- ½ cup hazelnut chocolate spread
- 1½ cups organic smooth peanut butter
- 1 cup white choc chips
- 12 cookies n crèmes biscuits (crushed)
- Pretzels (for dipping)

Directions:

1. Melt together the hazelnut chocolate spread, peanut butter, and choc chips using a microwave. Stir until silky and allow to cool.

2. Stir in the crushed biscuits until incorporated.

3. Serve at room temperature with pretzels.

Pumpkin Pie Choc Chip Cheesecake Dip

A whole new way to get your pumpkin pie fix! This dip is almost too good to share.

Servings: 4-6

Total Time: 10mins

Ingredients:

- 2 cups powdered sugar
- 8 ounces full-fat cream cheese (at room temperature)
- 3 tsp pumpkin pie spice
- 15 ounces canned organic pumpkin
- 1 tsp vanilla essence
- 1 cup 50% cocoa choc chips

Directions:

1. Beat together the powdered sugar and cream cheese in a mixing bowl.

2. Mix in the pumpkin pie spice, pumpkin, and vanilla.

3. Fold in the choc chips until incorporated.

4. Serve straight away,

Truffles and Treats

Cabernet Chocolate Truffles

An after-dinner nibble, or party pleaser; these red wine-infused truffles are amazing.

Servings: 30

Total Time: 2hours 30mins

Ingredients:

- 5 ounces milk chocolate (chopped)
- 5 ounces dark chocolate (chopped3/4 cup heavy cream)
- ¾ cup heavy cream
- 3 tbsp. cabernet sauvignon
- Cocoa powder (to roll)

Directions:

1. Add the chocolates to a large mixing bowl.

2. In saucepan over moderate heat, heat the heavy cream. As soon as the cream comes to a boil, take the pan off the heat and pour it over the chocolate in the bowl.

3. Add the cabernet sauvignon and allow to rest for a few minutes, before whisking until silky smooth.

4. Add a piece of plastic kitchen wrap over the top of the mixing bowl, and press it down so that it sticks to the chocolate.

5. Transfer to the fridge for a couple of hours.

6. Next, using a melon baller scoop the chocolate out and roll into balls. Transfer to a sheet of parchment.

7. Finally, roll each truffle in cocoa powder and then transfer to the fridge for half an hour.

8. Serve chilled.

Champagne Celebration Truffles

The next time you are getting ready for a big celebration, whip up a batch of these fancy champagne chocolate truffles. They also make a great food gift.

Servings: 24

Total Time: 11hours 30mins

Ingredients:

Truffles:

- 8 ounces good quality semisweet choc chips
- ½ cup heavy cream
- ¼ cup + 2 tbsp. Prosecco or Champagne

Coating:

- 16 ounces dark choc chips
- Edible gold decorations

Directions:

1. Add the choc chips to a bowl and set aside.

2. Boil the cream in a small saucepan over moderate heat, immediately pour over the choc chips. Allow to stand for a couple of minutes before stirring until silky.

3. Carefully stir in the Champagne. Cover and chill overnight.

4. Use a melon baller to scoop a little truffle mixture at a time and use your hands to roll into a smooth ball.

5. Chill for an hour.

6. Melt the dark choc chips using a microwave, stir until silky.

7. Cover a cookie sheet with wax paper.

8. Using toothpicks dip each chilled truffle in the melted chocolate and place on the cookie sheet.

9. Sprinkle over your chosen nonpareils. Chill for 2-3 hours before serving.

Cherry Crisp Treats with Dark Chocolate

Chewy cherry treats for the whole family to enjoy.

Servings: 24-30

Total Time: 1hour 10mins

Ingredients:

- 6 tbsp. butter
- 1½ tbsp. cherry gelatin powder
- 1 (16 ounce) pack mini pink and white mallows
- 8 cups crisped rice cereal
- 11 ounces dark chocolate (melted)

Directions:

1. Ina pan, melt the butter along with the cherry gelatin powder, and mini mallows over low heat, while continually stirring until the mallows are smooth and melted.

2. Fold in the rice cereal and gently press the mixture into a lightly buttered cookie sheet of approximately 13x9".

3. Frost the treats with the melted chocolate and allow to set for an hour.

4. Cut into even squares and enjoy.

Chocolate and Jasmine Tea-Time Truffles

It's time for tea and what better to go with a hot brew than these Jasmine tea infused truffles?

Servings: 20

Total Time: 2hours 45mins

Ingredients:

- 4 ounces semisweet chocolate (finely chopped)
- 1½ tbsp. unsalted butter (cut into small pieces)
- Pinch of salt
- ¾ cup water
- ¾ ounce premium jasmine green tea leaves
- 6 tbsp. heavy cream
- Unsweetened cocoa powder

Directions:

1. In a medium mixing bowl, combine the finely chopped chocolate with the butter and a pinch of salt.

2. In a small pan, bring the water and jasmine tea to a boil.

3. Strain the tea into a small bowl, pressing down on the leaves to extract as much tea as you can.

4. Pour the tea back into the pan, add the heavy cream and bring to boil, pour the mixture over the chocolate mixture, whisking until silky smooth.

5. Allow to cool for half an hour.

6. Press a sheet of plastic kitchen wrap directly onto the surface of the chocolate and place in the fridge for a couple of hours.

7. Using a teaspoon, shape the chocolate into small balls before rolling all over in unsweetened cocoa powder.

8. Enjoy.

Chocolate Bacon Truffles

Sometimes opposites attract, and this is the case with these homemade truffles, salty bacon combines with sweet chocolate.

Servings: 40

Total Time: 1hour 30mins

Ingredients:

- 1¼ cups dark chocolate peanut butter
- ½ cup butter (melted)
- 3 cups confectioner's sugar
- 1 tsp vanilla essence
- 1 (16 ounce) package chocolate coating
- 8 rashers cooked bacon (finely chopped)

Directions:

1. In a large mixing bowl, mix the dark chocolate peanut butter, butter, confectioners' sugar and vanilla essence.

2. Roll the mixture into small balls and transfer to the fridge for 30-60 minutes.

3. Melt the chocolate coating according to the package instructions.

4. Dip each truffle in the chocolate coating, allow any excess to fall off.

5. Place the truffles on parchment paper and scatter with diced bacon.

Chocolate Drizzled Cherry Mallow Crispies

Crunchy, cherry mallow squares are topped with milk chocolate for pop in the mouth treats that are totally addictive.

Servings: 24

Total Time: 30mins

Ingredients:

- 4 tbsp. salted butter
- 1 (10 ounce) bag mini mallows
- 4 ounces cherry jello powder
- 6 cups crisp rice cereal
- 1½ cups milk choc chips
- 1 tbsp. shortening

Directions:

1. Melt together the butter and mallows in a saucepan over moderate heat.

2. Stir in the cherry jello powder.

3. Take off the heat and stir in the cereal until totally coated and combined.

4. Press the mixture into a rimmed baking sheet. Allow to cool.

5. Melt the choc chips and shortening together using a double boiler. Stir until silky and drizzle over the cooled mixture in the sheet.

6. Allow to cool and set before slicing into small squares.

Dark Chocolate Maple Syrup and Coconut Treats

Whichever chocolate holiday you decide to celebrate this dark chocolate treat is sure to be a party pleaser.

Servings: 12

Total Time: 1hour 45mins

Ingredients:

Coconut Filling:

- 2½ cups unsweetened organic coconut (finely shredded)
- ½ cup coconut oil (melted)
- ¼ cup maple syrup
- 1 tsp vanilla essence

Chocolate Topping:

- 6 ounces 100% unsweetened organic dark chocolate
- 1 tbsp. coconut oil
- ⅓ cup maple syrup

Directions:

1. In a mixing bowl, combine all of the coconut filling ingredients; the organic coconut, coconut oil, maple syrup, and vanilla essence and mix thoroughly until incorporated.

2. Evenly divide the filling mixture between a 12-cup muffin pan, pressing to make sure the mixture is even. Transfer the pan to the freezer, and freeze for half an hour, until hard.

3. In the meantime, and while the filling is cooling, in a double boiler, melt the dark chocolate together with the coconut oil.

4. Once melted, whisk until totally combined, take the pan off the heat and add the maple syrup. Stir to incorporate.

5. Remove the muffin pan from the freezer, and evenly dived the chocolate mixture over each cup, spooning on top and smoothing out to make sure that it sufficiently covers the coconut.

6. Return the pan to your freezer, for 30-45 minutes, or until set.

7. To free the treats from the pan, carefully slide a knife around the rim of the treat, and pop out.

8. Store in the fridge until ready to eat.

Pistachio Nut Crispy Bars with Dark Chocolate

Crispy squares aren't just for kids, this pistachio nut and dark chocolate version will please the grownups too!

Servings: 16

Total Time: 3hours

Ingredients:

- Butter (for greasing)
- 12 ounces crisp rice cereal
- ½ cup pistachio nuts (roughly chopped)
- 6 tbsp. butter
- 16 ounces large mallows
- ½ tbsp. sea salt
- 2 cups semi sweet choc chips
- 2 tbsp. virgin coconut oil

Directions:

1. Grease a rectangular baking pan.

2. Add the cereal and nuts to a mixing bowl, set to one side.

3. Melt together the butter and mallows in a saucepan over moderate heat. Stir well.

4. Pour the mixture over the cereal. Use a spatula to mix until combined.

5. Press the mixture into the baking pan and chill for half an hour.

6. Sprinkle with the sea salt.

7. Chill for half an hour and slice into bars.

8. Melt together the choc chips and coconut oil using a microwave. Stir until silky.

9. Cover a cookie sheet with wax paper.

10. Dip one end of each bar in the melted chocolate and place on the cookie sheet.

11. Chill for a couple of hours before serving.

Red Velvet Cake Truffles

Bite into dark chocolate truffles to reveal red velvet cake.

Servings: 40

Total Time: 3hours

Ingredients:

- 1 (15½ ounce) box red velvet cake mix*
- 8 ounces low-fat cream cheese (softened)
- 12 ounces milk choc chips
- 2 tsp vegetable oil

Directions:

1. First, prepare the red velvet cake according to the box directions. Allow to completely cool.

2. Using clean hands, carefully, over a mixing bowl, break the cake up into fine crumb. Add the softened cream cheese and with your hands, gently knead until fully combined.

3. Roll the mixture into 40 balls and place on a cookie sheet lined with wax paper.

4. Transfer to the fridge to chill.

5. In the meantime, melt the chocolate in a double boiler, stirring until combined.

6. Add the vegetable oil, and stir to incorporate.

7. Take the cake balls out of the refrigeration and one ball at a time, place in the melted chocolate.

8. Using a metal fork, evenly coat each of the balls in the chocolate.

9. Use the fork to remove the truffles from the chocolate and transfer them back to the cookies sheet, while lightly tapping the fork against the bowl to remove excess chocolate.

10. Place the balls on the cookie sheet and repeat the process until all of the balls are on the sheet.

11. Pour the remaining leftover melted chocolate into a zip lock bag, using kitchen scissors cut one corner of the bag off and pipe the chocolate in your preferred design.

12. Return the truffles to the refrigerator for 15-30 minutes until set.

*You will also need the ingredients to prepare the cake mix; these are listed on the box.

Violet White Chocolate Ruffles

Indulgent white chocolate and delicate floral violet is a match made in heaven. Family and friends will be seriously impressed.

Servings: 32

Total Time: 11hours 15mins

Ingredients:

- 5 ounces good quality white choc chips
- ⅓ + 2 tbsp. heavy cream
- 1 tsp violet essence
- Candied violet petals (to decorate)

Directions:

1. Add the choc chips and half of the heavy cream to a saucepan. Bring to a gentle boil. Take off the heat straight away and allow to cool for a few minutes before stirring in the remaining cream and essence.

2. Chill overnight.

3. Transfer the chilled ganache to a stand mixer and whip until fluffy.

4. Transfer to a frosting bag with a ruffle tip and pipe ruffles into small cupcake liners.

5. Decorate each ruffle with a candied violet petal.

6. Chill for 2-3 hours before serving.

White Chocolate Matzo Cracker Treats

Super simple, even the kids can join in making these treats.

Servings: 6

Total Time: 40mins

Ingredients:

- 2 matzo crackers
- ¾ cup white chocolate chips
- Rainbow sprinkles

Directions:

1. Line a cooking sheet with parchment and set to one side.

2. Break the crackers into 3 vertical pieces and arrange them on the cookie sheet.

3. In a double boiler melt the chocolate, stirring until smooth.

4. While holding one end of the cracker, dip the bottom third into the melted chocolate, allowing any excess to fall, as you lift it out of the chocolate.

5. Return the dipped crackers to the cookie sheet, scatter with sprinkles and allow to dry on the cookie sheet for half an hour, at room temperature.

Zesty Lemon White Chocolate Truffles

Thanks to lemon zest and oil these truffles are bursting with zingy lemon flavor while sweet white chocolate makes them melt in the mouth creamy.

Servings: 32

Total Time: 4hours

Ingredients:

- 2 tbsp. butter (at room temperature)
- 10 ounces good quality white choc chips
- 1 tsp light corn syrup
- 6 tbsp. heavy cream
- ½ lemon (zested)
- 1 drop lemon oil
- Sugar (for rolling)

Directions:

1. Using a double boiler, melt together the butter and choc chips. Stir until silky. Set to one side.

2. Over moderate heat, combine the corn syrup and heavy cream in a saucepan. When the mixture begins to gently bubble, immediately pour over the melted white chocolate mixture. Stir for a few minutes, then add the lemon zest and oil. Keep stirring until smooth. Chill for a few hours until firm.

3. Scoop a little of the truffle mixture at a time using a small melon baller and roll into smooth balls.

4. Coat each ball in sugar.

5. Chill for half an hour before serving.

Author's Afterthoughts

Thanks ever so much to each of my cherished readers for investing the time to read this book!

I know you could have picked from many other books but you chose this one. So a big thanks for downloading this book and reading all the way to the end.

If you enjoyed this book or received value from it, I'd like to ask you for a favor. Please take a few minutes to post an honest and heartfelt review on Amazon.com. Your support does make a difference and helps to benefit other people.

Thanks!

Daniel Humphreys

About the Author

Daniel Humphreys

Many people will ask me if I am German or Norman, and my answer is that I am 100% unique! Joking aside, I owe my cooking influence mainly to my mother who was British! I can certainly make a mean Sheppard's pie, but when it comes to preparing Bratwurst sausages and drinking beer with friends, I am also all in!

I am taking you on this culinary journey with me and hope you can appreciate my diversified background. In my 15 years career as a chef, I never had a dish returned to me by one of clients, so that should say something about me! Actually, I will take that back. My worst critic is my four years old son, who refuses to taste anything that is green color. That shall pass, I am sure.

My hope is to help my children discover the joy of cooking and sharing their creations with their loved ones, like I did all my life. When you develop a passion for cooking and my suspicious is that you have one as well, it usually sticks for life. The best advice I can give anyone as a professional chef is invest. Invest your time, your heart in each meal you are creating. Invest also a little money in good cooking hardware and quality ingredients. But most of all enjoy every meal you prepare with YOUR friends and family!

Made in the USA
Las Vegas, NV
07 July 2021